Real Madrid CF

Kate Shoup

New York

Published in 2020 by Cavendish Square Publishing, LLC
243 5th Avenue, Suite 136, New York, NY 10016

Copyright © 2020 by Cavendish Square Publishing, LLC

First Edition

No part of this publication may be reproduced, stored in a retrieval system, or transmitted in any form or by any means—electronic, mechanical, photocopying, recording, or otherwise—without the prior permission of the copyright owner. Request for permission should be addressed to Permissions, Cavendish Square Publishing, 243 5th Avenue, Suite 136, New York, NY 10016. Tel (877) 980-4450; fax (877) 980-4454.

Website: cavendishsq.com

This publication represents the opinions and views of the author based on his or her personal experience, knowledge, and research. The information in this book serves as a general guide only. The author and publisher have used their best efforts in preparing this book and disclaim liability rising directly or indirectly from the use and application of this book.

All websites were available and accurate when this book was sent to press.

Library of Congress Cataloging-in-Publication Data

Names: Shoup, Kate, 1972- author.
Title: Real Madrid CF / Kate Shoup.
Description: First Edition. | New York : Cavendish Square, 2020. | Series: Soccer's greatest clubs | Includes bibliographical references and index. | Audience: Grade level for this book is grades 5-8.
Identifiers: LCCN 2019010642 (print) | LCCN 2019019541 (ebook) | ISBN 9781502652621 (library bound : alk. paper) | ISBN 9781502652614 (paperback : alk. paper)
Subjects: LCSH: Real Madrid Club de Fútbol--History--Juvenile literature.
Classification: LCC GV943.6.R35 S56 2020 (print) | LCC GV943.6.R35 (ebook) | DDC 796.334/64094641--dc23
LC record available at https://lccn.loc.gov/2019010642
LC ebook record available at https://lccn.loc.gov/2019019541

Editor: Kristen Susienka
Copy Editor: Rebecca Rohan
Associate Art Director: Alan Sliwinski
Designer: Jessica Nevins
Production Coordinator: Karol Szymczuk
Photo Research: J8 Media

The photographs in this book are used by permission and through the courtesy of: Cover Jose Brenton/Pics Action/Shutterstock.com; p. 1 (and used throughout) Soccer ball - Focus Stocker/Shutterstock.com, Emblem - Onur Cem/Shutterstock.com, Grass - Comzeal Images/Shutterstock.com; p. 4 Laurence Griffiths/Getty Images; p. 6 Pictorial Press Ltd/Alamy Stock Photo; p. 7 Popperfoto/Getty Images; p. 9 Gabriel Bouys/AFP/Getty Images; p. 10 Keystone-France/Gamma-Keystone/Getty Images; p. 12 Denis Doyle/Getty Images; p. 15 Bettmann/Getty Images; p. 18 Dominique Berretty/Gamma-Rapho/Getty Images; p. 23 Album/Alamy Stock Photo; p. 24 Gianni Ferrari/Cover/Getty Images; p. 25 Wikimedia Commons/File:Di-stefano.jpg/Public Domain; p. 26 Burak Akbulut/Anadolu Agency/Getty Images; p. 29 Emilio Cobos/EB/Getty Images; p. 31 David Ramos/Getty Images; p. 35 Power Sport Images/Getty Images; p. 36 Domenico Stinellis/AP Images; p. 38 David S. Bustamante/Soccrates/Getty Images; p. 41 Denis Doyle/Getty Images; p. 42 Javier Soriano/AFP/Getty Images; p. 45 Gonzalo Arroyo Moreno/Getty Images; p. 46 Pablo Blazquez Dominguez/Getty Images; p. 49 Chris Brunskill Ltd/Getty Images; p. 50 Quality Sport Images/Getty Images; p. 52 Angel Martinez/Real Madrid/Getty Images.

Printed in the United States of America

TABLE OF CONTENTS

Chapter 1:
Soccer and Real Madrid's Origins. 5

Chapter 2:
A Century of Real Madrid 13

Chapter 3:
Hauling in the Hardware 27

Chapter 4:
Modern Challenges 37

Chapter 5:
The Legacy of Real Madrid 47

Chronology 53
Glossary 55
Further Information 58
Selected Bibliography 60
Index 62
About the Author 64

Real Madrid players raise the Champions League trophy after winning in 2016.

SOCCER AND REAL MADRID'S ORIGINS

The game that Americans call soccer but almost everyone else calls football is a ball game played by two teams on a rectangular field with a goal on each end. This field is called a pitch. The object of the game is to get the ball in the other team's goal. Each team's goal is protected by a player called a goalkeeper, or goalie.

SOCCER EXPLAINED

Only the goalie can touch the ball with his or her hands or arms. No other players are allowed to do this. Instead, they move the ball by kicking it with their feet. They also use their legs, knees, chests, and even their heads to move the ball.

The team with the most goals at the end of a game, or match, wins. If both teams score the same number of goals, the match typically ends in a draw, or tie. If the match is part of a knockout tournament, however, then it will go into overtime or a shootout. In a shootout, both teams take five penalty kicks. A penalty kick is when a player takes a single shot on goal with only the other team's goalie to defend it. Whichever team scores the most goals during the shootout wins the game.

THE HISTORY OF SOCCER

No one knows for sure when soccer started. According to the sport's international governing body, the Fédération Internationale de Football Association (FIFA), "A search down the centuries reveals at least half a dozen different games ... to which the historical development of football has been traced back." However, one thing is clear: thousands of people around the world have enjoyed the sport, or simply kicking a ball to each other, for centuries.

People in Europe and other parts of the world have enjoyed kicking a ball around for hundreds of years.

6 Real Madrid CF

Members of the Royal Engineers Football Club are shown here in 1872. Soccer uniforms back then looked very different!

We do know that in 1863, soccer officially split off from another popular game, called rugby football. People had been playing the new game that would become soccer for a while, and it was beginning to gain popularity. The split occurred when members of several sporting clubs in London, England, met to define the rules of the new game. This included how many players could be on the pitch, the size and weight of the ball, whether carrying the ball was allowed, and so on. The

SPORT SHORT
According to the *Oxford English Dictionary*, the word soccer is an abbreviation of the word "association" plus the suffix "-er."

Soccer and Real Madrid's Origins   **7**

group also created a new organization to govern the game's play, called the Football Association (FA).

This new form of football became known as association football to tell it apart from rugby football. Association football quickly attracted attention. In just eight years, the number of British football clubs affiliated with the FA jumped from eleven to fifty. The FA organized the world's first-ever "knockout" association football tournament in 1872 and launched a league championship in 1888. The FA remains the governing body of association football in England today.

REAL MADRID: A WINNING TRADITION

In 1897, a group of association football fans in Madrid, Spain, began meeting once a week to play the game. Since then, this club has become one of the top soccer teams in Spain and in all of Europe. In fact, the Madridistas, as they're affectionately called, have positively dominated the competition. They've won thirty-three championships in Spain's national league (La Liga) and thirteen in the top European league (Champions League) as of 2019. No other club has even come close.

SPORT SHORT
Madrid Club de Fútbol was founded in 1902. Its name today is Real Madrid Club de Fútbol (CF). It is more than one hundred years old.

Real Madrid player Gareth Bale (*center*) heads the ball during a game against Club Atlético de Madrid in 2019.

MADRIDISMO AND *MACHACAR*

The club's excellent record is connected to one of its favorite ideas: Madridismo. Real Madrid club president Florentino Perez defines Madridismo as "courage, leadership, desire, solidarity among the players and respect for your rivals." Spanish journalist Luis Gómez lists the main elements of Madridismo as "a sense of … hard work, humility, and honesty."

Says author Brian Boedker, "Real Madrid is a club of winners." This winning attitude is perhaps best summed up by another Spanish phrase: *machacar*. This phrase started in bullfighting and translates roughly to "crush without mercy." Just as a bullfighter, or matador, must end a bullfight before the bull ends him, "Real Madrid

Francisco Franco hands the European Cup to Real Madrid team captain Miguel Muñoz in 1957.

doesn't let its opponents off the hook, even if they are ahead 7–0," says Boedker. Players for Real Madrid are expected to keep going, no matter what, until they've defeated the other team.

A COMPLEX HISTORY ... AND A BRIGHT FUTURE

No sporting organization is "just a team." Each one has its own special history. Real Madrid's history is connected to that of Spain—most notably with a brutal fascist dictator named Francisco Franco. Franco ruled Spain from 1939 until his death in 1975. He used Real Madrid to promote his regime.

A "ROYAL" CLUB

Before Real Madrid was connected to Franco, the club was associated with Spanish King Alfonso XIII, who became king at age sixteen in 1902. This was the same year Real Madrid was formed. The king enjoyed watching games and was the inspiration for adding "Real" (or "Royal") to the team's name in 1920.

Today, the club's association with Franco is seen as a bad part of its history. This is especially true among fans of the club's archrival, Barcelona. Many people in Barcelona were against Franco. Some Barcelona fans even believe that Real Madrid was successful during Franco's time only because of Franco's support.

Regardless, these days, Real Madrid very clearly stands on its own. In the 2010s, it's won two La Liga titles and four Champions League championships. Not only that, but it's the richest soccer club in the world. Its success is a result of hardworking management and determined players.

Teammates Sergio Ramos (*right*) and Cristiano Ronaldo (*left*) jump for the ball at a home game in 2014.

A CENTURY OF REAL MADRID

During the late 1800s, British people living in Spain began creating soccer clubs there. The first of these was in a town called Huelva, near the coast. It was founded in 1889. Similar clubs were founded in Bilbao (1898) and Barcelona (1899).

THE BIRTH OF A SOCCER TEAM

In 1897, British and Spanish students at a college in Madrid started a soccer club of their own. It was called Foot-Ball Sky. Every Sunday, the group met to play games together.

The club's first president was also a player. His name was Julian Palacios. Palacios described early Foot-Ball Sky games:

> *When I played at center-forward I tried to make life as difficult as possible for defenders, but they left their marks on me as well. We had referees sometimes, but few of them agreed on the rules. They all had their own versions of the game,*

A Century of Real Madrid   13

and frankly it was easier to play without them ... Sky had a goalkeeper who used to sit on a chair in front of the goal-line drinking lemonade and just relaxing. When we attacked, he used to jump up and throw the chair behind the line, and put on this really serious expression.

Not everyone was so laid-back. One Englishman, named Arthur Johnson, was quite intense. Palacios recalled:

The only guy who really knew what he was doing back then was the Englishman Johnson. Lovely chap, too, but he took the game very seriously. He got married here in Madrid on a Saturday, and turned up to play the match on the following morning. I don't know what his bride thought.

In 1900, Foot-Ball Sky split into two new clubs: New Foot-Ball de Madrid and Madrid Club de Fútbol (or Football Club in English). Eventually, New Foot-Ball de Madrid fell away. Only Madrid Football Club remained. On March 6, 1902, Madrid Football Club became "official." Members agreed on club rules, elected a board of directors, and registered with local authorities.

SPORT SHORT

Arthur Johnson was the first player to score a goal for Madrid Club de Fútbol in official competition in 1902.

They also decided that the members would make all the business decisions and would own the club. Finally, they elected a new president. His name was Juan Padrós. Padrós came from Barcelona. Fútbol Club Barcelona, often called Barça, would quickly become Madrid Football Club's archnemesis.

THE COPA DEL REY

In May 1902, five Spanish soccer clubs met in Madrid for the first national soccer tournament. These clubs were Madrid Football Club, New Foot-Ball de Madrid, Fútbol Club Barcelona, Club Español de Foot-Ball, and Club Bizcaya. The knockout tournament was played to celebrate the recent coronation, or crowning, of Spanish King Alfonso XIII. It was called the Copa de Coronación (Coronation Cup). Club Bizcaya defeated Fútbol Club Barcelona in the final game to win the cup. So many fans packed Madrid's stadium for the final game that workmen built extra wooden bleachers to make sure everyone had a seat.

King Alfonso XIII of Spain was an early supporter of soccer and of Real Madrid.

After that, the tournament was held every year. It was renamed the Copa del Rey (King's Cup). It is still played today. Madrid Football Club won its first Copa del Rey in 1905.

King Alfonso was patron of several Spanish teams, including Madrid

A Century of Real Madrid   15

SPORT SHORT
Madrid Club de Fútbol played Fútbol Club Barcelona for the first time during the Copa de Coronación. Barcelona won 3–1.

Football Club. It was in his honor that the club added "Real" to its name in 1920.

STARTING THE SPANISH FOOTBALL FEDERATION AND LA LIGA

In response to the sport's growing popularity, several top clubs, including Madrid Football Club, joined to form the Federación Española de Fútbol (Spanish Football Federation) in 1909. This became the sport's governing body in Spain and remains so today—although its name is now the Real Federación Española de Fútbol (RFEF). In 1913, the Spanish Football Federation joined FIFA, which was created in 1904. It is soccer's international governing body.

Twenty years later, the Spanish Football Federation launched its own championship league, the Campeonato Nacional de Liga de Primera División (National Championship League First Division). This league is more commonly known as La Liga. It originally had ten clubs, including Real Madrid and Fútbol Club Barcelona. The league followed a round-robin format, with each of the ten clubs playing every other club twice—once at home and once away—for a total of eighteen games. "Such a campaign seems short now," observes writer Phil Ball in *White Storm: 101 Years of Real Madrid*. "But one suspects that back then, with [older] training methods, poorer diets and total lack of medical back-up, it was long enough." It used a point system to decide the league champion. Clubs were given three points for a win, one point for a tie, and zero points for a loss. Whichever club had the most points at the end of the season won the title. La Liga uses the same round-robin and points format today but has twenty clubs rather than ten.

Real Madrid finished second in La Liga that first year, after Fútbol Club Barcelona. It was not until the 1931–1932 season that the Madridistas would win the title. They won it again in 1932–1933. By this time, play had become quite serious. Goalies no longer sat "on a chair in front of the goal-line drinking lemonade and just relaxing." Clubs tried to attract top players and paid them well.

THE SPANISH CIVIL WAR

Spain became a unified country in 1492. Until 1833, it was ruled by a series of kings and queens. In 1833, Spain became a constitutional monarchy. This meant its king or queen shared power with a lawmaking group called parliament. Members of parliament were elected by the people.

In 1923, a Spanish military man named Miguel Primo de Rivera got rid of parliament and took over as dictator. King Alfonso XIII, who had tried to get rid of parliament himself, supported de Rivera.

By 1930, Spain's economy was failing, and de Rivera had become very unpopular. He was forced out of his role. King Alfonso's own fall wasn't far behind. Elections in 1931 resulted in huge wins for candidates who were against the monarchy. They wrote a new constitution and formed a republic. This new republic was called the Second Spanish Republic. Stripped of his power, King Alfonso fled to Rome, Italy. He remained there for the rest of his life.

   A group led by a Spanish military general named Francisco Franco did not like the new republican government. In July 1936, they tried to take it over. This was the beginning of the Spanish Civil War. Over the next three years, Franco's fighters beat republican forces to take over Spain. The war ended after they captured Barcelona in January 1939 and Madrid in March 1939.

   After beating the republicans, Franco became dictator of Spain. He proclaimed himself El Caudillo, or head of state and government. He held this position until his death in 1975.

   The Spanish Civil War was a difficult time in Spain's history. Two hundred thousand soldiers died fighting in it. In addition to these, tens of thousands of people died when Franco bombed Spanish cities or while fleeing to other parts of Europe. That wasn't all. There were also nearly two hundred thousand people who were targeted and killed because of their

Francisco Franco gives a salute in 1967.

political ideas. Others died in concentration camps in Spain.

During the Spanish Civil War, all La Liga play stopped. (It started again in December 1939.) The Madrid Football Club, which had dropped the "Real" from its name in 1931 after King Alfonso XIII left Spain and the Second Spanish Republic formed, basically closed its doors. Franco's forces murdered the club's vice president and treasurer, as well as a former player named Ramon "Monchín" Triana. Another former player was almost killed too: a goalkeeper named Ricardo Zamora, who was a prisoner during the war. "He was going to be taken out of the prison with a group of prisoners, surely to be shot, when he was recognized by a soldier who saved his life," one of his sons later said.

THE "REGIME TEAM"

Although Spain became a unified country in 1492, each part has its own culture and language. To strengthen his power, Franco did not let people in different regions express their culture or even speak their language. Sometimes he punished people violently. "One Spain great and free," was Franco's motto. However, many people were not free.

Franco used soccer to push his ideas on other people. He eventually supported Real Madrid (which restored the "Real" to its name in 1943 with Franco's blessing) as a statement against rival clubs in problem regions. These included Fútbol Club Barcelona in Catalonia and Atlético Bilbao in Basque. As a result, says soccer journalist Aakriti Mehrotra, Real Madrid became "a perfect personification of his fascist leadership." For its part, Fútbol Club Barcelona turned into "the symbol of republican resistance, against Franco's oppressive regime and its oppression of the Catalan culture."

Some Fútbol Club Barcelona fans suggest that Real Madrid's success on the pitch was because of Franco's support. In the case of the 1943 Copa del Rey tournament, that may have been true. However, it would be a mistake to say that Real Madrid was great because of Franco's support. Rather, "Franco supported them because they were great," says journalist Nick Fitzgerald. "Real Madrid symbolized everything that Franco stood for."

Franco didn't use soccer just to punish problem regions. He also used it to distract the people of Spain from his repressive and sometimes brutal policies. "In times of unrest and unhappiness with the regime," says journalist Callum Connolly, "Franco would broadcast games live throughout Spain … the Spanish people would become so preoccupied with the entertainment that they would ignore everything else, much to Franco's benefit."

Finally, Franco used soccer to improve Spain's reputation in Europe and elsewhere through international play. Indeed, Real Madrid's success on the world stage during the 1950s and 1960s prompted Spain's foreign minister at the time to describe the club as "the best embassy we ever had."

"El Caudillo's utilization of sport to attain his objectives was unrivalled by any leader, past or present," says Connolly. "Francisco Franco's rule may

EL CLÁSICO: REAL MADRID VS. BARCELONA

Real Madrid and Fútbol Club Barcelona were rivals long before Franco. However, Franco's rise brought their rivalry to a new level. Today, that rivalry continues. Indeed, says sportswriter Dan Rookwood, the two clubs "hate each other with the bitter intensity of 1,000 pickled lemons."

The rivalry, called El Clásico, really heated up when the two clubs met in the semifinals during the 1943 Copa del Rey tournament. Before the game, Franco's security chief made a surprise visit to the Barcelona team. "Do not forget that some of you are only playing because of the generosity of the regime that has forgiven you for your lack of patriotism," the chief said. The men got the message. Fearing for their lives, the Fútbol Club Barcelona players simply stood by as Real Madrid scored a whopping eleven goals.

Since then, the ill feelings between the two squads have only increased. This has made El Clásico one of the most heated rivalries in all of sports. No matter where they play, the stadium is always full, and millions of people watch the games on TV.

have been oppressive and bleak, but it was ruthlessly efficient thanks to football."

MANY STADIUMS, ONE TEAM

Before 1947, Real Madrid played its games on a few different pitches. The club's first dedicated stadium was the Campo de O'Donnell. Built in 1912, it held just two hundred spectators.

Before long, the club outgrew the Campo de O'Donnell. In 1923, it moved to a new home, a velodrome with space for eight thousand fans, called the Campo de Ciudad Lineal. Just one year later, the club moved again—this time to a stadium with room for fifteen thousand spectators. It was called the Estadio Chamartín, after the district in which it was built.

The Spanish Civil War left its mark on Chamartín. Indeed, the stadium was "all but destroyed," says Phil Ball, "its wooden stands converted into fuel." Although volunteer workers managed to put the building back together, the club's president, Santiago Bernabéu, realized that "the folks who mattered were not going to turn up every fortnight [two weeks] to some broken-down ruin of a stadium," says Ball. Bernabéu arranged for a new stadium to be built. It would be next door to the old one. It was named Santiago Bernabéu Stadium, or simply, the Bernabéu. It held a crowd of seventy-five thousand. It is still the home of Real Madrid today.

TOP PLAYERS

Despite Franco's support of Real Madrid after the Spanish Civil War, the club's playing was far from

Santiago Bernabéu Stadium is home to Real Madrid.

perfect. Between 1939 and 1952, the club failed to win a single La Liga championship and won only two Copas del Rey.

It began to get better when a new player from Argentina named Alfredo di Stéfano joined in 1953. Called la Saeta Rubio (the Blond Arrow), di Stéfano could play "under any conditions in any position," says Phil Ball. Between 1953 and 1964, he led the club to eight La Liga championships, one Copa del Rey, and five European titles.

Di Stéfano was just one of many excellent players to wear a Real Madrid jersey. Another was Emilio Butragueño, who played for Real Madrid from 1984 to 1995. Nicknamed el Buitre (the Vulture), Butragueño was famous for "being in the right place, then reacting with the minimum of fuss," says Ball—"a flick here, a chip there, quiet little efforts that became his killer's trademark."

A Century of Real Madrid   23

REAL MADRID'S MAIN MANAGER: SANTIAGO BERNABÉU

Santiago Bernabéu was born in 1895 to a middle-class family in a small Spanish town called Almansa. When he was six years old, his family moved to Madrid.

As a young boy, Bernabéu became a big supporter of Real Madrid. He went to the games often. In 1909, at the age of fourteen, he joined the club's youth team as a striker. He was later promoted to the main team and even served as captain before retiring from play in 1927.

Santiago Bernabéu (*left*) stands with coach Miguel Muñoz (*right*) in 1973.

Bernabéu took on many roles—director, assistant manager, manager of the main squad—before being elected club president in 1943. He was president until his death in 1978.

Bernabéu brought several of the club's most famous players to the team and oversaw its incredible growth. This was thanks in part to Franco's support—something Bernabéu, who had fought under Franco during the Spanish Civil War, almost certainly used to his advantage. "Politics aside," says Phil Ball, "there had never been anyone quite like him, and we have certainly not seen his like since."

Raúl González—a native of Madrid whose time on the team lasted from 1994 to 2010—was also successful. In fact, his talent and skill made him *so* famous that fans called him simply "Raúl." Joining Raúl was another one-name wonder, an Argentinian named Redondo, who played from 1994 to 2000.

Four very big names joined the team in the early 2000s. The first was Portuguese midfielder Luís Figo. He joined in 2000 and remained until 2005. Next came French midfielder Zinedine Zidane. He arrived in 2001 and stayed until 2006. (He also was the club's head coach starting in 2016.) Joining this duo was Brazilian striker Ronaldo. His time with the club began in 2002 and lasted until 2007. Finally, British midfielder David Beckham arrived in 2003 and left in 2007. Together, they were called los Galácticos (the Superstars).

More star players followed, including Kaká (who played from 2009 to 2013), Cristiano Ronaldo (who played from 2009 to 2018), and Gareth Bale (who joined the club in 2013 and still is on the team as of summer 2019). With a group like this, it's no wonder the club has been so successful at home and away.

The legendary Alfredo di Stéfano played for Real Madrid during the 1950s and 1960s.

A Century of Real Madrid

Real Madrid players celebrate their 2017 La Liga championship win with head coach Zinedine Zidane (*right*).

HAULING IN THE HARDWARE

Real Madrid is a soccer team that has won a lot. From its start through 2019, Real Madrid has won thirteen Champions League trophies and thirty-three La Liga championship titles. That is the most of any club. It's also received nineteen Copas del Rey—third after Fútbol Club Barcelona (who have won thirty) and Atlético Bilbao (who have won twenty-three).

SUCCESS IN SPAIN

Often, the club has won a lot in several years close together. Between 1905 and 1908, the club won four Copas del Rey in a row. During the 1980s, it claimed five straight La Liga titles. More impressive were the nine La Liga titles in ten seasons, from 1953 to 1964. Even when the club doesn't win, it's nearly always one of the best teams. It's finished second in La Liga standings twenty-three times and been runner-up for the Copa del Rey twenty times.

As of 2019, Real Madrid's most recent La Liga championship was in 2017. That season, the club won twenty-nine games in the Spanish league, lost six, and

SPORT SHORT
During the rule of Francisco Franco, the Copa del Rey was called the Copa del Generalíssimo. Generalíssimo was a name for Franco.

tied three. It scored an impressive ninety-three points. As of summer 2019, Real Madrid last won the Copa del Rey in 2014. Even though its top goal scorer, Cristiano Ronaldo, was out that day because of knee and thigh injuries, Real Madrid beat Fútbol Club Barcelona 2–1. This was thanks to a great goal by Gareth Bale with five minutes left.

TRIUMPH IN UEFA

During the early 1950s, Real Madrid president Santiago Bernabéu encouraged starting a new yearly soccer tournament for top European clubs. It was called the European Cup. The European Cup was an idea from the late 1940s by French journalists Gabriel Hanot and Jacques Ferran. The tournament would be managed by a new organization called the Union of European Football Associations (UEFA). UEFA was formed to manage the national soccer associations in Europe—including the Spanish Football Federation. UEFA is part of FIFA.

The main purpose of the European Cup was to allow European clubs to come up with a team hierarchy, or list. However, the tournament served another purpose: helping heal hurts caused during World War II. Sixteen clubs on both sides of that conflict participated in the

REAL MADRID BALONCESTO

Real Madrid is more than a soccer club. It's also a basketball club: Real Madrid Baloncesto.

Just as Real Madrid Club de Fútbol has had great success in La Liga, Real Madrid Baloncesto has been at the top of its league. Since its founding in 1931, Real Madrid Baloncesto has won thirty-four championships. It won seven straight between 1960 and 1966 and ten in a row from 1968 to 1977. Also, the club has won twenty-seven Copas del Rey de Baloncestos—including one in 2017.

Real Madrid Baloncesto is one of Europe's top basketball clubs.

The club has also done great in games against international teams. A typical favorite in Europe's top basketball league, called the EuroLeague, Real Madrid Baloncesto has won a record ten championships in this international league as of summer 2019.

first tournament. These included squads from Italy, West Germany, Austria, Poland, Hungary, Yugoslavia, Netherlands, Belgium, France, and Scotland, plus Denmark, Sweden, Switzerland, Portugal, and Spain.

For Spanish dictator Francisco Franco, the idea of a new European tournament was particularly appealing. This was because the tournament would help improve Spain's image in Europe. "Franco's regime, although primarily inward-looking, was hugely concerned with the way it was perceived by the rest of Europe," writes football journalist Nick Fitzgerald. Spanish soccer clubs—particularly Real Madrid—were "the perfect PR tool, projecting the idea of a wealthy, happy and united Spain that was at odds with the reality."

The first European Cup was in 1956. Real Madrid won. That was the first of five straight European Cup wins under the leadership of Alfredo di Stéfano—the last of these in 1960. Real Madrid won a sixth European Cup in 1966 with an all-Spanish team. The Spanish newspapers called this group the Yé-Yés after several players posed for photos wearing Beatles wigs. The name was referring to the popular Beatles song "She Loves You." It has the lyrics "Yeah, Yeah, Yeah" in its chorus. Real Madrid has won the European Cup seven more times as of 2019.

In 1993, UEFA changed the name of the European Cup to the Champions League. Today, thirty-two clubs take part in the Champions League tournament. Clubs are selected based on their ranking within their national league. Stronger national leagues are given more spots in the tournament. As of 2019, La Liga is ranked highest among the national leagues. This means there are more

Gareth Bale (*center*) celebrates his game-winning goal against Liverpool to claim the 2018 Champions League title.

Spanish teams in the Champions League tournament than from any other country.

OTHER TOURNAMENT WINS

The winner of the Champions League plays in another important international competition called the FIFA Club World Cup. As of 2019, Real Madrid has won the FIFA Club World Cup four times, in 2014, 2016, 2017, and 2018. No other team has matched that number.

As winner of the Champions League tournament, Real Madrid also competed in the UEFA Super Cup. The UEFA Super Cup is a game between the winner of the Champions League and the top club in the Europa

SPORT SHORT
Between 2016 and 2018, Real Madrid won three straight Champions League titles.

League. The Europa League is also run by UEFA. It is one level below the Champions League. As of 2019, Real Madrid has won the UEFA Super Cup four times, in 2002, 2014, 2016, and 2017.

Real Madrid has also won the Europa League twice. This statistic is probably one most players and fans would rather forget, however. This is because the Europa League is not UEFA's top league.

Between 1960 and 2004, there was another important game called the International Cup. This was played by the top Champions League team and the top team from the Confederación Sudamericana de Fútbol (the South American Football Confederation). Real Madrid won this cup three times, in 1960, 1998, and 2002.

THE WILDERNESS YEARS

There have been low points too. Real Madrid has even come close to relegation—being dropped out of its league. The Royal Spanish Football Federation oversees an organization called the Liga de Fútbol Profesional (Professional Football League, or LFP). The LFP has forty-two clubs, grouped into two divisions: the Primera División (the famous La Liga) and the Segunda División (called La Liga 2). Only the top twenty clubs in the LFP play in La Liga; the rest compete in La Liga 2. At the end of each season, the three lowest-placing clubs in La Liga are relegated to La Liga 2—replaced by the top two clubs in La Liga 2 and the winner of a playoff game. Real Madrid narrowly avoided this fate in the 1948–1949 season but has never come close to it since. In fact, Real Madrid is one of just three original members of La Liga never to face relegation. (The other two are Fútbol Club Barcelona and Atlético Bilbao.)

The truth is, Real Madrid's so-called "bad years" would be great years for most other clubs. Take the period between 1967 and 1997. During this time, the club won sixteen La Liga championships and seven Copas del Rey. However, because it failed to win a single Champions League title, the club and its fans view this time as a low period. There's even a name for it, la Época del Desierto (or the Wilderness Years).

BALLON D'OR AND GOLDEN SHOE HONORS

Since 1956, a popular French magazine called *France Football* has celebrated the top player in Europe each year with a trophy called the Ballon d'Or (Golden Ball). Several Real Madrid players have won this award.

The first member of the Real Madrid team to win the Ballon d'Or was Alfredo di Stéfano. He won the trophy twice, in 1957 and again in 1959. Di Stéfano also won the Super Ballon d'Or in 1989. The Super Ballon d'Or was a one-time trophy that recognized the best player to ever play in Europe at that time. Another Real Madrid player named Raymond Kopa won the Ballon d'Or in 1958.

THE REAL MADRID FOUNDATION

In 1997, Real Madrid started the Real Madrid Foundation. The charity works to help make sure soccer and other sports become part of every child's life. This group has helped thousands of children around the world. The Real Madrid Foundation also encourages the use of sports to help all people at all ages, anywhere. Finally, it joins with other charities to raise money after natural disasters or other bad things happen in the world.

In 2011, it joined with a group called the United Nations Relief and Works Agency (UNRWA). They sent coaches and sports equipment to Palestine. Children living in refugee camps there got a chance to exercise and have fun in a safe place. As of 2016, nearly 1,200 children had taken part in the program.

Despite Real Madrid's success on the field, it would be forty-one years before another Madridista won the Ballon d'Or. This time, a creative Portuguese midfielder named Luís Figo won it. Two years later, Brazilian player Ronaldo won. This was, in fact, Ronaldo's second Ballon d'Or. He won his first one in 1997 while playing for a club in Italy called Football Club Internazionale Milano.

Cristiano Ronaldo appears with some of his Ballon d'Or trophies in 2018.

An Italian defender named Fabio Cannavaro came next, winning in 2006.

Between 2013 and 2017, Real Madrid forward Cristiano Ronaldo won an astonishing four Ballons d'Or. These were in addition to the Ballon d'Or he won in 2008 while playing for Manchester United. In 2018, another Real Madrid player, Croatian midfielder Luka Modrić, hauled in the hardware.

The European Golden Shoe (sometimes called the Golden Boot) is another famous soccer trophy. It goes to the player who scores the most goals in European league competition. Between the award's start in 1968 and 2019, it has been won by two Real Madrid players: Hugo Sánchez in 1990 and Cristiano Ronaldo in 2011, 2014, and 2015.

Los Galácticos included soccer stars like Luís Figo (*left*), Ronaldo (*center*), and Zinedine Zidane (*right*).

MODERN CHALLENGES

When Real Madrid was founded, it was a tiny club. Most members were players, and they paid to be on the team and play. Fast-forward one hundred years, and things have changed! Real Madrid is no longer a just-for-fun club for soccer fans. Now, it's one of the most successful, most popular, and most powerful sports teams in the world. However, its success has also brought challenges.

MONEY AND ATTRACTING TOP TALENT

As mentioned, during the early 2000s, Real Madrid recruited several big-name soccer stars. These included Luís Figo (2000–2005), Zinedine Zidane (2001–2006), Ronaldo (2002–2007), David Beckham (2003–2007), and others. The Spanish newspapers called this famous group of players los Galácticos, or the Superstars. Los Galácticos were very talented. They were also *extremely* expensive—they cost a lot of money every year.

On top of player salaries, soccer clubs often must pay another fee to have players who are with other clubs join their team. This fee is called a transfer fee. Transfer fees are often large sums of money. For example, to obtain Figo, Real Madrid paid Barcelona €62 million ($70.3 million); Zidane cost €77.5 million ($87.9 million); and Ronaldo cost €17 million ($19.2 million).

Paying these large salaries and transfer fees put Real Madrid deeply in debt. To address this problem, club president Florentino Pérez—who served in this role from 2000 to 2006 and again from 2009 to the present—sold some expensive real estate owned by the club. This canceled its debts. Pérez then came up with a new plan to make sure the club had financial success in the future. He would make it more attractive to players and fans. This involved making the team into

Real Madrid president Florentino Pérez has put the club on solid financial footing.

a brand. Pérez saw the club as being like a Hollywood movie. Signing top players like Figo, Zidane, Ronaldo, and Beckham would help bring more fans and players to the club the same way casting Harrison Ford or Jennifer Lawrence in a movie helps bring people to the movie theaters.

Pérez's plan worked. According to *Forbes* magazine, Real Madrid is now worth more than $4 billion and draws an annual revenue of $735 million. In 2017, a company called Brand Finance, which assesses the value of sports brands, called Real Madrid the most powerful soccer brand in the world and the second most valuable (after Manchester United).

This economic achievement has brought sporting success. It has also drawn even bigger (and more expensive) stars to the squad. Cristiano Ronaldo joined Real Madrid in 2009 and played for nine seasons, at a total cost of more than €200 million ($226.8 million) in salary plus a record-breaking €97 million ($109.9 million) transfer fee. Gareth Bale signed on in 2013 for another high transfer fee and salary.

COURTING SPONSORS

Sports teams need help from other organizations to survive. Lots of times, these organizations work with the team to advertise. They might give the team money to have signs or announcements about the organization during games. These organizations are called sponsors. Building relationships with sponsors isn't easy, but it helps the team continue to run successfully and pay its players.

WHO OWNS REAL MADRID?

Real Madrid has an interesting business model. It's owned by its fans. Club owners are called socios *(members). Fútbol Club Barcelona, Atlético Bilbao, and Osasuna have a similar arrangement.*

At first, Real Madrid had only a handful of members. Today, the club has over one hundred thousand members. Each member pays a membership fee.

Socios over the age of eighteen can vote in elections for club officers, such as the club president and the board of directors. Some members can also run in these elections. In addition, members can buy season tickets (depending on availability).

One good thing about this model is that it helps build a bond between the club and its community. The fact that the club president is elected by club members makes it more likely that the president will run the club in a responsible manner. It's an unusual model, but it works.

Real Madrid has two main sponsors. One of these is a Dubai-based airline named Emirates. Since 2013, Emirates has been Real Madrid's main shirt sponsor. This means the Emirates logo appears on each player's jersey. Large images of Real Madrid players also appear

Sponsors help Real Madrid succeed on the field. Here, players wear the jersey with sponsor Emirates's logo while holding trophies.

on several Emirates planes. For the exposure, the airline currently pays the club a sum of €70 million ($79 million) per year.

Adidas is another main sponsor. This popular sporting goods company has produced the club's kit, or uniform, since 1998. In 2018, Adidas extended its relationship with Real Madrid until 2028. Real Madrid also has deals with several other sponsors, including Nivea Men, Audi, EA Sports, and Coca-Cola.

FINDING NEW FANS

In Spain, people either like Real Madrid or they don't. It's becoming harder to draw more fans in from other European countries. Many Europeans are fans of other

SPORT SHORT
The Real Madrid home uniform consists of white shorts and a white jersey. The away uniform is typically either all blue or all purple.

teams in their own countries. To get more fans, Real Madrid needs to look to countries farther away.

In the twenty-first century, the club has done just that. They've tried to get new fans in China, Japan, South Korea, and the Middle East, as well as the United States, Canada, and South America. The results have been impressive. According to a 2018 article in the *Nikkei Asian Review*, "Nearly 250 million of Real Madrid's more than 600 million fans worldwide hail from the Asia-Pacific region."

Real Madrid has also begun playing matches in these regions—particularly in the United States. In

Real Madrid has hundreds of millions of fans all over the world.

2018, the squad played a match against English team Manchester United in Miami, Florida.

Real Madrid connects with its fans using social media. As of 2019, the club has more than 50 million Twitter followers, nearly 70 million Instagram followers, and almost 110 million Facebook fans.

HANDLING HOOLIGANISM

Real Madrid works hard to get more people interested in the club. However, there's one group of fans that causes trouble. They're called the Ultras Sur. This group is noisy, disruptive, and even violent during matches.

This kind of behavior from soccer fans is called hooliganism. It's a common problem for soccer clubs. It has been around for a long time, even as early as the 1300s.

The Ultras Sur haven't been around *quite* that long. The group was founded in the 1980s. This was a time of change in Spain from a terrible rule under Franco to a fully democratic society. The founding members of the Ultras Sur didn't like this change. In fact, they liked Real Madrid because of the club's ties to Franco.

During home matches, the group gathered behind the goal on the south end of Santiago Bernabéu Stadium. (This explains their name, because *sur* means "south" in Spanish.) They sang rude songs and waved

SPORT SHORT
Real Madrid's main nickname is Los Blancos (The Whites) because of their all-white home uniform.

Modern Challenges 43

OTHER RIVALRIES

Fútbol Club Barcelona might be Real Madrid's biggest rival. However, it's not the only one. Real Madrid has other smaller rivalries in both La Liga and the UEFA Champions League.

One smaller La Liga rival plays just across town—Atlético Madrid. When Real Madrid plays Atlético Madrid, the match is called El Derbi Madrileño (The Madrid Derby). The Madrid Derby is about more than sports. It's a clash of cultures: Real Madrid, which represents the reportedly more well-off, against Atlético Madrid, which represents the working class.

Internationally, a rivalry has developed between Real Madrid and Bayern Munich. This is because both squads have been very successful in the Champions League and are quite evenly matched. Of twenty-six matches played as of 2019, Real Madrid has won twelve, Bayern Munich has won eleven, and three have ended in a tie.

offensive flags. They also shouted at and bullied players of color. Sometimes, they were even violent.

For too long, Real Madrid put up with the Ultras Sur, but by 2013, the club had enough. It fined certain members of this group and banned the group from the stadium. Real Madrid also gave the group's seats to

The Ultras Sur engaged in hooliganism and even violence before being banned by Real Madrid.

a different group of fans called the Grada. According to the Grada's website, the purpose of the Grada is to celebrate in the stadium "without violence, politics, racism and intolerance" and "with only one feeling: MADRIDISMO!"

Unfortunately, the Ultras Sur haven't gone away completely. As recently as October 2018, a group of Ultras Sur was arrested outside the stadium. This happened right before El Derbi Madrileño (The Madrid Derby). However, club president Florentino Pérez vowed to keep them out. He will continue to do what he can to not let that kind of behavior happen near the club.

FIFA named Real Madrid the top club of the twentieth century with this award.

THE LEGACY OF REAL MADRID

Today, Real Madrid is one of the world's top soccer clubs. In the twentieth and twenty-first centuries, it has earned many awards. This helps people know how important the club is in soccer's history.

In 2010, the International Federation of Football History and Statistics declared it the European club of the twentieth century. FIFA went one step farther, naming it the number one club of the twentieth century out of all soccer clubs around the world. FIFA also awarded the club a Centennial Order of Merit—its highest honor.

Clearly, Real Madrid has earned this praise. Its thirty-three La Liga titles as of 2019 are eight more than any other club. Real Madrid has also dominated Champions League play, earning six more titles than the runner-up as of 2019. Also, only Fútbol Club Barcelona and Atlético Bilbao have won more Copas del Rey than Real Madrid.

THE CLUB OF THE TWENTIETH CENTURY … AND BEYOND?

Being called the club of the twentieth century is a big deal. However, Real Madrid also wants to have a good reputation in the twenty-first century. Fortunately, at least for now, things are going well. The year 2017 was a very good one. That was the year the club won La Liga, the Champions League, and the FIFA Club World Cup. It also won the European Super Cup—a contest between the winner of the Champions League and the UEFA Europa League. Finally, it captured the Supercopa de España (Spanish Super Cup)—a mini-tournament that features the winner and runner-up of La Liga and the finalists in the Copa del Rey. Real Madrid calls 2017 its "best season in history."

GROWING THE NEXT GENERATION

In 2018, Real Madrid superstar Cristiano Ronaldo left for another club, called Juventus, in Italy. "I believe the time has come to start a new era in my life," he explained in a letter to Real Madrid fans. That left a big hole in the Real Madrid lineup.

So, what's next for Real Madrid? For the moment, the club is in a rebuilding phase. Club favorites Gareth Bale and Luka Modrić remain with the club as of 2019. If they leave, then it will be up to young players like Spanish midfielder Dani Ceballos, Spanish fullback Álvaro Odriozola, Brazilian forward Vinícius Júnior, and Spanish midfielder Marco Asensio to take over

Coach Zinedine Zidane (*right*) congratulates Cristiano Ronaldo (*left*) after winning the 2018 Champions League.

and shine. Of course, the club could always sign more star players.

The club has another source for fresh players. Since the 1950s, it has supported a youth academy that trains promising players called La Fábrica (The Factory). Real Madrid scouts from La Fábrica travel the world looking for new talent—some as young as ten years old. Players who are selected are invited to move to Madrid for coaching at the academy. Some of the kids even live there. More than 270 young players currently practice at La Fábrica.

Life at La Fábrica is hard. The pressure is intense. Competitiveness is encouraged. "Our club ethos is *nunca se rinde* (never give up)," says coach Javier Morán. He explains that players "need to be a certain

The Legacy of Real Madrid   49

Brazilian forward Vinícius Júnior is a key young player on the Real Madrid squad.

kind of individual to succeed here … they need that competitive edge to achieve their targets."

La Fábrica offers top training facilities. There are twelve outdoor pitches and four swimming pools. The gym, says sportswriter Richard Fitzpatrick, "is easily as long as a … cross-field pass." For the boys who live at La Fábrica, there are fun places, too, like game rooms and movie theaters. The young athletes are responsible for bringing their own soccer cleats, but the academy provides everything else in terms of gear.

La Fábrica has produced its share of top Real Madrid players. Emilio Butragueño was one. Raúl was another. A third was Iker Casillas. He was the club's goalie from 1999 to 2015 and is considered one of the

> **SPORT SHORT**
> Since the 1950s, 179 La Fábrica players have gone on to play in La Liga. Thirty-two of these have played for Real Madrid as of 2019.

best goalkeepers ever. Other academy graduates have played on other La Liga teams. According to Fitzgerald, during the 2016 season, "41 players from La Fábrica are playing with squads in the premier division of La Liga." An additional 28 appeared on club rosters in La Liga 2. Still, the boys training at La Fábrica know their odds of playing at the highest levels are slim.

One thing is for sure: whether by signing current superstars or growing their own, Real Madrid will most likely be one of the top clubs for the rest of this century and beyond.

BUILDING A NEW STADIUM

In addition to signing top players, the club is building a new and modern stadium to make players and fans more comfortable. "It'll be the best stadium in the world," says club president Florentino Peréz.

The new stadium will have special walls "which can be lit up and upon which images can be projected," the club says. This stadium's overall design, says its architect Volkwin Marg, was "inspired by medieval cathedrals, with all their sculptures and paintings around the building telling their stories."

A retractable roof will cover the pitch and seating areas, in case there's bad weather, and a 360-degree

A model of Real Madrid's new stadium shows a retractable roof.

scoreboard will let fans in every corner of the place view the action at all times. The museum that displays the club's trophies and cups will also be redone, and a new shopping center will be added. Outside the stadium, a new walking zone will make it more accessible to fans.

These changes won't be cheap. It's estimated the new stadium will cost €525 million ($595 million), but Pérez says it will quickly pay for itself. Each season, it's expected to bring in an extra €150 million ($179 million). Construction began in spring 2019 and will take three-and-a-half years to complete.

With its new stadium, top players, healthy bank account, and smart management team, the future of Real Madrid looks bright.

CHRONOLOGY

1897 A group of association football enthusiasts in Madrid form a club called Foot-Ball Sky.

1900 Foot-Ball Sky splits into two new clubs: New Foot-Ball de Madrid and Madrid Football Club.

1902 Madrid Football Club is "officially" formed. The first Copa del Rey is played in Madrid.

1905 Madrid Football Club wins its first Copa del Rey.

1909 The Spanish Football Federation is formed.

1920 Madrid Football Club changes its name to Real Madrid.

1929 The Spanish Football Federation starts a national football league called La Liga.

1932 Real Madrid wins its first La Liga title.

1936– 1939 The Spanish Civil War happens. La Liga play is suspended during this period. It resumes in December 1939.

1939 Francisco Franco becomes dictator of Spain.

1943 Santiago Bernabéu is elected club president.

1947 Santiago Bernabéu Stadium is built.

1949   Real Madrid narrowly avoids relegation.

1953   Real Madrid signs Alfredo di Stéfano.

1956   Real Madrid wins the first of five consecutive Champions League titles.

2000   Florentino Pérez becomes president, and the Galácticos era begins.

2009   Real Madrid signs Cristiano Ronaldo.

2013   Florentino Pérez bans the Ultras Sur from Bernabéu Stadium.

2016   Real Madrid wins the first of three consecutive Champions League titles.

2018   Star player Cristiano Ronaldo leaves the club.

2019   Real Madrid enters a rebuilding phase.

GLOSSARY

association football The sport that is more commonly called football or soccer.

concentration camp A place that gathers prisoners in one area, often used to hold political opponents and other people seen as undesirable by a brutal government.

constitutional monarchy A type of government in which a king or queen rules within limits of a constitution.

defender A player on a soccer team who plays closest to his or her team's goal. Defenders help the goalie protect the goal.

dictator A political leader who has complete control over a country.

fascist Relating to a form of government characterized by strict rule and bad treatment of certain groups or opponents.

forward A player on a soccer team who plays closest to the other team's goal. Forwards generally score more goals than players in other positions.

found To start or create.

goalkeeper The player on a soccer team who protects the team's goal. Another word for goalkeeper is goalie.

hooligan An unruly football fan.

kit Another word for soccer uniform.

knockout tournament A tournament format in which the winner of the match advances to the next round but the loser is knocked out.

machacar A Spanish word that translates roughly to "crush without mercy." This word has its roots in bullfighting.

Madridismo A word that describes the spirit of Real Madrid. Spanish journalist Luis Gómez defines Madridismo as "a sense of austerity, hard work, humility and honesty."

Madridista Another name for Real Madrid or for a player on or fan of the team.

match A soccer game.

midfielder A player on a soccer team who plays in the middle of the field, between the team's forwards and defenders.

oppression The strict control or unjust treatment of a certain person or group.

penalty kick A free kick awarded when a foul by the defending team occurs inside the penalty box. The ball is placed twelve yards from goal with only the opposing team's goalie to defend it.

pitch The field on which a soccer match is played.

regime A harsh government.

relegation The demotion of a soccer club from one level in the club's league to the level below it.

retractable Able to be pulled back or pulled in.

round-robin A tournament format in which every competitor plays every other competitor at least once.

semifinal A game or round in a tournament immediately before the final game. The winner of a semifinal goes on to play in the final.

socio A member and part owner of a soccer club such as the Real Madrid Football Club.

sponsor A company or other organization that forms a relationship with a team; sponsors pay money to help support the team, and in exchange, the team might put the sponsor's logo on its jerseys or near the field of play.

striker The player on a soccer team whose main job is to score goals. The striker typically plays at the center-forward position.

transfer fee A fee paid between soccer clubs to get a player who is under contract with one club to join a different team. Transfer fees often cost a lot of money.

FURTHER INFORMATION

BOOKS

Ball, Phil. *White Storm: The Story of Real Madrid*. Edinburgh, Scotland, UK: Mainstream Sport, 2003.

Fitzpatrick, Richard. *El Clásico: Barcelona v Real Madrid: Football's Greatest Rivalry*. New York, NY: Bloomsbury USA, 2013.

Whiting, Jim. *Soccer Stars: Real Madrid*. Mankato, MN: Creative Paperbacks, 2017.

Wilson, Paula M. *Inside Professional Soccer: Real Madrid*. Calgary, Alberta, Canada: Weigl Educational Publishers Ltd., 2018.

WEBSITES

La Liga
https://www.laliga.es/en
This is the official English-language La Liga website.

MARCA Real Madrid
https://www.marca.com/en/football/real-madrid.html
This site features Real Madrid news from *MARCA*—a Spanish daily sports newspaper.

Real Madrid
https://www.realmadrid.com/en
This is the official English-language website of Real Madrid.

UEFA Champions League
https://www.uefa.com/uefachampionsleague/index.html
Get the latest news about the Champions League here.

VIDEOS
The Best Season in History
https://www.realmadrid.com/en/news/2017/06/the-best-season-in-history
This video contains top clips from 2017—the team's best season yet.

How the Spanish Civil War Shaped El Clásico: Real Madrid vs Barcelona
https://www.youtube.com/watch?v=2WpkS9AUdLY
This video discusses the roots of the El Clásico rivalry.

115 Years of Legend
https://www.realmadrid.com/en/news/2017/03/115-years-of-legend
This video celebrates 115 years of Real Madrid Football Club and Real Madrid Baloncesto.

SELECTED BIBLIOGRAPHY

Ball, Phil. "Mucho Morbo." *Guardian*, April 21, 2002. Accessed February 18, 2019. https://www.theguardian.com/football/2002/apr/21/championsleague.sport.

Ball, Phil. *White Storm: 101 Years of Real Madrid*. Edinburgh, UK: Mainstream Publishing Company, 2002.

Callejo, Miguel Blanco, and Francisco Javier Forcadell. "Real Madrid Football Club: A New Model of Business Organization for Sports Clubs in Spain." *Global Business and Organizational Excellence* 51–64. 2006.

Clapham, Alex. "Inside Real Madrid's Academy: 'Only a Certain Type of Person Succeeds Here'." *Guardian*, March 21, 2018. Accessed February 21, 2019. https://www.theguardian.com/football/2018/mar/21/real-madrid-academy-city-spain-barcelona-la-fabrica.

Fitzpatrick, Richard. "The Secrets of La Fabrica: Inside Real Madrid's Academy, Where Winning Is Everything and Only the Strongest Survive." Bleacherreport.com, November 3, 2016. Accessed February 21, 2019. https://thelab.bleacherreport.com/the-secrets-of-la-fabrica.

Hochschild, Adam. "Process of Extermination." *New York Times*, May 11, 2012: BR32.

Ingle, Sean, and Mark Hodgkinson. "When Did Football Hooliganism Start?" *Guardian*, December 13, 2001. Accessed February 21, 2019. https://www.theguardian.com/football/2001/dec/13/theknowledge.sport.

Khan, Khalid. "Cure or Curse: Socio Club Ownerships in Spanish La Liga." Bleacherreport.com, June 11, 2010. Accessed February 20, 2019. https://bleacherreport.com/articles/404511-cure-or-curse-socio-club-ownerships-in-spanish-la-liga.

Mehrotra, Aakriti. "Fascism & Football: The Political History of Spanish Football." *Outside of the Boot*, Accessed February 19, 2019. http://outsideoftheboot.com/2014/05/22/fascism-football-the-political-history-of-spanish-football.

"Police Arrest 27 Real Madrid Ultras Armed with Knuckle Dusters and Sticks Before the Derby." AS.com, October 4, 2018. Accessed February 21, 2019. https://en.as.com/en/2018/10/03/football/1538580499_681471.html.

"Real Madrid Aims to Score with Chinese Sponsors and Fans." May 26, 2018. Accessed January 21, 2019. https://asia.nikkei.com/Business/Companies/Real-Madrid-aims-to-score-with-Chinese-sponsors-and-fans.

Ronaldo, Cristiano. "Cristiano Ronaldo's Goodbye Letter to Real Madrid Fans in Full." Sport-English.com, October 7, 2018. Accessed February 21, 2019. https://www.sport-english.com/en/news/real-madrid/cristiano-ronaldos-goodbye-letter-to-real-madrid-fans-in-full-6935424.

Spain, Kevin. "Ronaldo Wins Ballon d'Or for Record-Tying Fifth Time." *USA Today*, December 7, 2017. Accessed February 20, 2019. https://www.usatoday.com/story/sports/soccer/2017/12/07/ronaldo-wins-ballon-dor-record-tying-fifth-time/931730001.

Srivastava, Nikhil. "Behind the Scenes at Real Madrid: How the Club Is Structured and How It Functions." Sports Keeda, August 3, 2015. Accessed February 20, 2019. https://www.sportskeeda.com/football/how-real-madrid-club-socios-president-elections-structure-functions.

Sung, Patrick, and Ben Church. "Real Madrid Planning 'the Best Stadium in the World' with $600 Million Facelift." CNN, October 31, 2018. Accessed February 21, 2019. https://www.cnn.com/2018/10/31/football/real-madrid-santiago-bernabeu-new-stadium-spt-intl/index.html.

Vargas, A. *La Verdadera Historia de Ricardo Zamora Durante la Guerra Civil Española,* January 30, 2012. Accessed February 18, 2019. https://guerraenmadrid.blogspot.com/search?q=zamora.

INDEX

Page numbers in **boldface** are images.

association football, 8
Atlético Bilbao, 13, 19, 27, 33, 40, 47

Bale, Gareth, **9**, 25, 28, **31**, 39, 48
Ballon d'Or, 33–35, **35**, **41**
Beckham, David, 25, 37, 39
Bernabéu, Santiago, 22, 24, **24**, 28

Champions League, **4**, 8, 11, 27, 30–33, **31**, 44, 47–48, **49**
concentration camp, 19
constitutional monarchy, 17
Copa del Rey, 15, 20–21, 23, 27–29, 33, 47–48

defender, 13, 35
di Stéfano, Alfredo, 23, **25**, 30, 33
dictator, 10, 17–18, 30
draw, 5

El Caudillo, 18, 20

European Cup, **10**, 28, 30

fascist, 10, 20
Fédération Internationale de Football Association (FIFA), 6, 16, 28, 47
FIFA Club World Cup, 31, 48
Football Association (FA), 8
forward, 13, 35, 48
Franco, Francisco, 10–11, **10**, 18–22, **18**, 24, 28, 30, 43
Futbol Club Barcelona, 11, 13, 15–21, 27–28, 33, 38, 40, 47

goalkeeper, 5, 14, 19, 50

hooligan, 43, **45**

King Alfonso XIII, 11, 15, **15**, 17–19
kit, 41
knockout tournament, 5, 8, 15

La Fábrica, 49–51
La Liga, 8, 11, 16–17, 19, 23, 27, 29–33, 44, 47–48, 50–51
los Galácticos, 25, **36**, 37

machacar, 9
Madridismo, 9, 45
Madridista, 8, 17, 34
Manchester United, 35, 43
match, 5, 14, 42–44
midfielder, 25, 34–35, 48

oppression, 20
overtime, 5

penalty kick, 5
Pérez, Florentino, 9, 38–39, **38**, 45, 51–52
pitch, 5, 7, 20, 22, 50–51

Real Federación Española de Fútbol (RFEF), 16
regime, 10, 20–21, 30
relegation, 32–33
retraction, 51, **52**
Ronaldo, 25, 34, 36, **37**, 39
Ronaldo, Cristiano, **12**, 25, 28, **35, 41,** 49
round-robin, 16–17

semifinal, 21
shootout, 5–6
socio, 40
Spanish Civil War, 17–19, 22, 24
sponsor, 39–41, **41**
striker, 24–25

transfer fee, 38–39

UEFA Super Cup, 31–32
Union of European Football Associations (UEFA), 28, 30, 32, 44, 48

Zidane, Zinedine, 25, **26**, **36**, 37–39, **49**

Index   63

ABOUT THE AUTHOR

Kate Shoup has written more than forty books and has edited hundreds more. When not working, Shoup loves to travel, watch IndyCar racing, ski, read, and ride her motorcycle. She lives in Indianapolis with her husband and their dog.